Darwin's Daughter

poems by
Faith Shearin

STEPHEN F. AUSTIN STATE UNIVERSITY PRESS 2017

For information about permission to reproduce selections from this book, contact *Permissions*, at sfapress@sfasu.edu

For information about special discounts for bulk purchases, contact *Distribution* at sfapress@sfasu.edu or 1-936-468-1078

Production Manager: Kimberly Verhine
Book Design: Jonathan Grant

For more information Contact:

STEPHEN F. AUSTIN STATE UNIVERSITY PRESS
414 Aikman Drive, LAN 203
P.O. BOX 13007
NACOGDOCHES, TEXAS 75962
sfapress@sfasu.edu
sfasu.edu/sfapress
936-468-1078

ISBN: 978-1-62288-164-2

Table of Contents

Acknowledgments

Several of the poems in this collection have appeared previously in the following journals, sometimes in slightly different form: "Our House, Surrounded by Animals" in *Slipstream;* "Mailing Babies" in *Burnside Review;* "White," "Sirens," and "Adam and Eve's Skeletons Found In Colorado" in *Common Ground Review;* "He Ate Peaches" and "No Windows" in *Tar River Poetry Review;* "The Great Moon Hoax" in *Cold Mountain Review;* "The Woman In The Viagra Commercial" in *Parody;* "Liminal States" in *Prime Number Magazine;* "Southern" and "Copperheads" in *Crosswinds;* "Bamboo Forest" in *Alaska Quarterly Review;* "Darwin's Daughter," "My Grandmother, Swimming," "My Mother, Getting Dressed," "Ruined Beauty," "Escapes," "Old Woman Returns to Rosebank Avenue," "Adam and Eve in Couples Therapy," "In This Photo of My Father," "Phrenology," and "Northwest Passage" in *Soundings East;* "Frances Glessner Lee" and "The Singing" in *Literal Latte;* "Potter's Field" in *Third Coast;* "One Sometimes Finds What One Is Not Looking For" in *Seminary Ridge Review;* "Jonestown," "A Pirate at Midlife," "1901 Portrait of Michael Fitzgibbons," "In 18 Century Britain," and "Deceased Child with Flowers" in *Sixfold;* Thank you to the Friday Writers: Melanie Sumner, Adrienne Su, Susan Mihalic, Wyatt Townley, and Tamara Powell. Thanks to Garrison Keillor for helping my work find its way into the world. Thanks to my family, immediate and extended: Mavis, Tom, Ruth, Anne, Norman, Dana, and Will. Thanks to the dogs, for sitting with me while I wrote: Gillyweed, Padfoot, Turtle, and Wookiee. Thanks to Sue Ann Devall for a year of advice, and for encouraging me to write.

"Bad things are going to happen./ Your tomatoes will grow a fungus/
and your cat will get run over."

> — Ellen Bass from *"Relax"*

"For years I had a happy childhood,/ if anyone asked I'd say, *it was happy.*"

> — Nick Flynn from *"The Captain Asks for a Show of Hands"*

In memory of my teacher, Thomas Lux, and for my father, Norman Shearin

Darwin's Daughter

Driving Home

Driving home on that December black
country road -- car lights,

stars -- I saw the fallen
deer in our lane, convulsing,

dying, but not yet dead, and I could not
swerve, but had to drive over,

chose to drive over, suffering:
ruined beauty, legs that had just

rushed through
trees, beyond farmhouses,

hooves thumping.

Snakebite

It was dusk when we opened the door and I have gone
back, many times, to try and close it. The dog

stepped out and shadows settled around her evening
walk, past stones and lupine, blooming blue

in our meadow. Even in my dreams the leaves
on our trees are the newest shade of green.

She was a puppy, so she suspected nothing.
She did not understand a creature so close

to the ground, traveling sideways, without legs.
It was dusk when we opened the door, then

darkness slithered.

Deceased Child With Flowers
after a memento mori

In this nineteenth century mourning portrait a child
has died and now lies in a formal bedroom beneath
wreaths of flowers. What we see is a face

on a pillow -- brown hair, long eyelashes --
and it is as if the tiny body is becoming a garden
of White Irises and Baby's Breath, as if grief

has erupted in blossoms and climbed the headboard,
as if the flowers in a nearby meadow
blew through a window and took root in this

mattress which is as soft as earth. There is
no sign, anymore, of fever or infection,
worry or doctors. The medicines, whatever

they were, vanished from the bedside table,
and now the child is becoming the flowers
which are also temporary: cut,

unable to drink, their petals tender.

Family Movies

No one has learned to hold the camera still
so there is an earthquake

in the white blur of these frames.
New babies are displayed on blankets

and sometimes couples wander
across mountainsides or beaches

without their heads. It is often Christmas
or someone's anniversary or a retirement

party where men are smoking cigars
and your grandmother walks through

the last years of her life in Florida,
beyond a hotel pool and a flock of flamingos,

to a sudden winter where snowmobiles
move in circles, carrying children

in orange suits. A tree glows in the window,
wrapped in tinsel, and the men are dressed up,

squinting into a kingdom of gifts.
An uncle falls in love with fall foliage

and a full hour passes,
in some lost Vermont October,

smoke seeping from chimneys;
then you step into the light, a hand

over your eyes, as if you can see us
out here, watching, in the uneaten cake

of the future.

Lucy, Falling

She dreamed in trees, scientists say,
and one night, three million years ago,

she fell: arms outstretched,
feet broken by a dry river bed.

Even now, Lucy slips through history,
plummets while the grassy

woodlands shiver. Our ancestor:
falling through time, after collecting fruit

or building a nest, her balance
unreliable. Lucy, who was dug up

near the fossilized remains of crocodiles
and crab claws, in Africa,

deep in some ancient lake;
terrestrial Lucy, vegetarian Lucy,

who becomes more human
as she loses her footing,

and lands alone and broken
on earth.

In This Photo of My Father

In this photo of my father he sits in a restaurant:
tea on the table, blue suit,

my sister across from him, and,
smiling, he has grown old.

It is morning, and the month before
he won his last supreme court case;

he has sold the sailboat, the piano,
the lot next door; once,

in earth science class, my teacher
explained the difference between submerging

and emerging coastlines, and I
drew a picture of our island

in my notebook, sinking. Everything
is temporary: the smile, the cup

of tea, half gone, the legal conference
where strangers have read

his argument and wait
to shake his hand. In Kindergarten

I drew a picture of my father carrying
a briefcase and his shoes were

also a crab's claws. I didn't know the name
for his profession, didn't understand

what he did behind his desk, where
his law books were open, like windows.

Sometimes, in his office,
a breeze moved through

the room, and we were
the island, and we were the sea.

My Mother At The Verizon Store

Before she agrees to sign a contract my mother asks
our salesperson, a boy named for a midwestern city,
what would happen to her phone service if she retired
to Ecuador and lived with endangered turtles;
she asks if her children would have to pay
the bill if she died, asks the boy
if he drinks Red Bull and, when he says no, asks
why people his age like it. My mother, breathless,

sways from side to side when she walks; she is
the oldest person in the Verizon store; inside her
purse: a notebook in which she has recorded,
in big cursive, the steps she must follow to send
a text. Afterwards, she spends the afternoon in bed,
watching black and white movies; *I understand
the past* she says. She misplaces the cord to her phone,
accidentally turns off its ringer, forgets how
to find her messages, watches as her power fades.

Emily Dickinson, Called Back

Emily lived fifteen years beside West Cemetery, watching
those solemn processions towards silence and, just before she died,

she wrote: *Dear cousins, called back.* Her casket was carried
by six Irish workmen and, following her instructions, they circled

her flower garden, walked through a horse barn,
took a grassy path through fields to a grave

lined with evergreen boughs, inside an iron fence;
she was called back the way children are called home

in the evenings, dusk falling over rooftops, wagons
and baseball bats abandoned in the grass, called back

the way dogs are called back from forests, their noses
pointed towards doorways.

Liminal States

We stand, then, on a threshold, in a doorway.
It is dusk or dawn and we have just awakened

from a deep sleep. I speak of the edges
between water and land, the place where

the forest gives way to a meadow, of the day
before my great grandfather died

when he stood in his fields, remembering.
This is just before the baby is born,

when it is time to push. The news
is coming but it has not arrived; I am

no longer young but I am not yet old.
My great grandmother believes her third son

will return from the war; my mother
is in the waiting room but no one has told

her she has cancer; my father's car
is spinning, but he is still conscious.

The cat in the nursing home who sleeps
with the one who is going to die is walking

silently down the white hallway
and he has not turned his head.

Just before we were married, we slept
with our rings on our fingers, imagining

how it would feel.

Escapes

Praise for the seven chimpanzees
at the Kansas City Zoo who fashioned

a ladder from branches; praise
for the eight monkeys in Brazil

who used stones to smash open
a lock. We need more penguins who

slide over thirteen foot walls
to plunge into Tokyo Bay. Let us

follow the example of Ken Allen,
the orangutan, who let himself

out of three difficult enclosures
then taught his friends how to open

their own gates. I want to be
the bobcat who leapt out of his

habitat -- man-made wall,
man-made moat -- to lie beside

a singing tree.

Frances Glessner Lee

She loved miniatures: made tiny replicas of rooms
that captured her imagination, recreated
the stiff chairs, the oil paintings of angels,
a pair of wire-rimmed glasses on a bedside table.

Frances spent her childhood reading Sherlock Holmes,
thinking about details, and later, after her marriage
collapsed, began making dioramas
of crime scenes: the angle of an opened door,

the way a body fell beside an ironing board,
while a nearby window came unlatched. She placed
ceramic figures on the mantle, hung coats
in closets, painted faint footprints on the floor.

Her family wouldn't allow her to study forensic pathology
then, one after another, they died, leaving
her a fortune. She funded Harvard's first homicide school,
lobbied to have coroners replaced by medical professionals,

hosted a conference where detectives looked into
her *Nutshell Studies of Unexplained Deaths*. I like
to think she recreated scenes from her own life too,
investigating personal crimes. Perhaps, in her attic,

she kept the miniature living room, with a polished mahogany
coffee table, where her father told her *A lady doesn't go
to school*. Or the dinner table where she cut her steak
while her husband criticized her understanding of the law.

Frances shrank the scenes so she could look into
them, and accuracy was important to her work.
In her rooms, calendars are turned to the right month
and year, rolling pins sit in flour, mouse traps

are poised to catch eyelash-sized mice. She recreated
the exact pallor and bloat of a rotting body, the splatter of blood
above a baby's crib. Is it any surprise that the victims
she considered were usually women, killed

in their own homes? She carved soap and shampoo
for the bathtub, stocked the kitchen pantry
with cereals, arranged soup cans,
opened an oven to reveal a pie.

Southern

It was the language I loved:
the way my great grandfather said the word
sassafras to amuse himself
and the aunties, surprised,
said *I swan* instead of *I swear.*
There, at the dinner table, eating
the biscuits and fried chicken
that will kill me, I heard
my first images and metaphors:
the oldest rat in this barn,
high cotton, down the country.
We aimed to do things; we reckoned
that we might. When a place was
far away it was *a fur piece* and
our anger moved through the room
on the legs of wet hens; our wishes
became horses; we were *like white*
on rice. It was the language,
in the heat, while mosquitoes
sang, and dangerous snakes
sunned themselves in our trees;
our dogs wouldn't hunt; our paintings
hung cattywampus on our walls.

Phrenology

This was a failed notion but a lovely one:
by measuring the bumps on the skull
you could find the bulked muscles
of the brain; there was once
a machine with spring-loaded
probes that made a map
of the mind. I have seen the drawings
from this era, the sculpted,
diagramed skulls. Each head had its own
topography like a planet; a large lump
at the back meant you were
designed for motherhood, while a lump
at the front gave you an appreciation
of beauty. Destructiveness lurked
above the ear, while delight in life
was tucked behind. Hope was on top,
between perseverance
and spirituality, just above a love
of the magnificent.

1901 Mourning Portrait of Michael Fitzgibbons
after the daguerreotype

I can make out a fence and two bare trees behind
the coffin which has been opened and propped upright
so the man inside stands, one last time,

beside his wife who is still young, squinting
into the future, with her hair tied in a knot,
a baby in her arms. The older children

are windblown and one turns her face
towards something unseen, outside the frame,
while her brother looks steadily into the distance,

unsmiling, choked by a tie. There is white
behind the dead man's head, and white
on the collars of his children; the baby's dress

is so white her mother holds her tightly
to keep her from floating away.

The Cures that Did Not Work

There were so many cures that did not work;
getting sick was dangerous, but medicine

was worse. All through history we bled ourselves
and drank mercury, treated dog bites

with earthworms and dung. We bored holes
in our skulls, hit cysts with books,

ate the powdered remains of mummies.
In ancient Greece a woman's womb

was a living animal that liked to wander;
to control the beast, girls married young

and bore many children. We took
Thalidomide for morning sickness,

smoked cigarettes to cure asthma,
bathed ourselves in urine. Illnesses were

demonic forces or punishments from God
and, during the plague, sinners marched

through the streets, whipping themselves;
doctors wore bird masks with beaks

half a foot long, filled with perfume.
We visited the sea for salt air

to cure our consumption, caught Malaria
to manage our Syphilis.

Mary Shelley, Creating Frankenstein

In a Swiss villa, during the gray rain of 1816, when
summer never came, Mary Shelley stayed

inside, reading. If you went back to those rooms
you would hear pages turning, tea cups

settling into saucers, the thunder
before the lightning in a wet, sunless gloom.

The writings of Erasmus Darwin
lay open on a table, his electricity

animating the darkness. Lanterns cast shadows;
volcanic ash fell like snow; young love

trembled in the night: Mary's
for Percy Shelley, her sister, Claire's

for Lord Byron; they competed
to tell the best ghost story and Mary invented

a pale physician kneeling
beside a creature he had stitched together

from grief. Death stole
Mary's mother one month after

she was born, then, three of her children,
in quick succession, and finally

Percy who launched
his boat in bad weather:

sails billowing into clouds.
In her imagination, Mary saw

how the physician was afraid of the corpse
he revived, how it followed him

into his bedchamber: opening curtains,
watching him with yellow eyes.

Eve, Growing Old

In paintings she stands, wrapped in her own hair,
or dressed in bits of foliage,
at the edge of a blooming paradise; she leans
towards a serpent, or touches a swollen fruit.
It wasn't enough that Eve was
the first woman, and therefore unmothered,
that God despised her curiosity,
that the knowledge she tasted was
really her own death. Next,
she grew old, older than anyone
you know: her bones thinning, her heart
filling more slowly, a strange ache
in her joints that was worse
before it rained. She held each
object at a distance and, still, she could not see;
she asked Adam to speak up. Why was
he mumbling? She could not quite remember
the name of a favorite animal. She slept horribly,
wandering through thorns, and she
was never the right temperature.
Her hair turned white, then fell out,
and she had no picture of her grandmother
on the bedside table to comfort her,
no ancestors waiting for her in myth,
or memory, no magnifying glass,
no trumpet for her ear.

My Father, Injecting Insulin

I tried not to look at his needles, arranged
in the refrigerator, growing cold,

or the injections themselves which my father
accomplished by pulling up his shirt tail

and stabbing his abdomen. I looked
away when he pricked his finger

at his desk, measuring sweetness,
focused instead on his jar of pencils,

though these were also hard and sharp,
waiting for words.

Darwin's Daughter

On the Galapagos Islands Darwin balanced
on the backs of giant tortoises, began
noticing variations: the way finches

were different at each port. It is said
that he lost his faith when he lost
his daughter, Annie, who liked

to look up words in dictionaries, her finger
drawn to names on maps;
she was ten when she died

that late April day, Darwin's
theory of evolution written
but still unpublished. Sundays,

during his later years, he went walking
in the forest while his family sat in church.
He believed that all life was related, descended

from a common ancestor, and he studied
his samples of plants and animals,
kept a yellow notebook, had a single

daguerreotype of his daughter in which she
did not smile, a basket of flowers
in her lap. He was a scientist and he wrote

his memories of Annie, folded
them into a labeled box; he described how
she touched his hair, how she sat
in his study, comparing two editions

of the same book, word by word.

He Ate Peaches

He ate peaches that last summer in the cabin
by the river where, each afternoon, I returned

from swimming to find him asleep
in a blue chair, his cane leaned against

a wall, my small dog in his lap.
Outside, on a picnic table, a pitcher

of sunlight was bathed in dew,
and when he opened his eyes my sister

began slicing peaches in the kitchen:
soft, downy swellings gathered in a basket.

My grandfather loved us and, being loved,
the days grew longer which is why I still believe

I will find him bent over a bowl as bright
as June, his hands shaking as he lifts

the fruit to his lips, knowing it is almost gone.

Family History

Uncles killed in the war lived
in attic photographs, fading

in their uniforms, the sound of their airplanes
over our picnics. Aunt Frances died of lung cancer,

her mouth pressed to a handkerchief, pale
in a summer cotton dress, while her brother Bill

felt something explode inside his mind. One grandfather
stopped breathing in his sleep, while the other

died walking through grocery store aisles, buying
ingredients for pie. All the aunties on my father's side

were diabetic, in their floral dresses, sipping tea,
their perfume too sweet. There was a suicide

after a stock market crash, a cousin who grew
thinner and thinner, until she disappeared.

One Sometimes Finds What One Is Not Looking For

Imagine Alexander Fleming returning to his lab
after a two week vacation; he was not
as tidy as some of the other scientists
and, while he was away, an open window
blew mold into his petri dishes; one,
blue and green, seemed to be eating
the bacteria that grew there. This was 1928
in London, where it often rains, and I
think sometimes of the window itself,
propped open because someone was hot,
or wanted air, and the sound of afternoon
thunderstorms. *One sometimes finds
what one is not looking for* Fleming said
after he named the mold penicillin,
and wrote a paper about it, saving
nearly everyone in my family at least once.
His lab was messy, I guess, which is how
the accident happened, and maybe
he was happy after his trip, dreaming
of oysters and cakes, some dappled afternoon
drinking tea beneath the trees; I praise
that open window, his mess, the mold
drifting in.

Guinevere, Praying

Gone was the table as round as a compass
and gone, too, the wizard, Merlin,
who climbed the Pine of Barenton,
hand over hand, up a ladder of branches,
had a great revelation, and never returned
to the mortal world again. After the last battle
at Camlann, King Arthur was placed in a barge
and sailed to the Isle of Avalon where
he drifted amid mists and apples,
tended by his sister, and Guinevere
went to live in a convent
near Stonehenge, love's fire behind her.
On her knees, hands clasped, she spent
the rest of her life in prayer: apologizing
for desire, Camelot flickering in her mind.
A black habit hid her hair and her room
was made of stone, her bed stiff. She was
bent, like my grandmother at the end,
over regret. Sometimes,
in dreams, Lancelot galloped past her:
his sword sharp, night burning.

Copperheads

Venomous vipers with a heat sensing pit
between nostril and eye: Death Adder,

Poplar Leaf, Chunk Head; they hide in stone walls
and sawdust, in wood piles, and gardens,

winter in dens with rattlers, sleeping
in piles of stripes. They liked to rise in early evening

that spring we nearly lost everything,
wriggle out of mountain caves where

they had been multiplying: fork-tongued,
hollow-fanged, planning ambush.

The Hobbits of Flores

Deep in a cave of the past we find
our tiny ancestors, on the island of Flores,
buried amid pygmy elephants,
and Komodo dragons, with their stone
tools and flat, sloping foreheads.
They stood three feet high, weighed
eighty pounds, had the faces
of men, but the wrists of apes.
We can see they built fires,
fed on fishes and lizards,
slept beside giant rats. I will let
the anthropologists argue about
whether or not they were deformed,
about the powers of a brain
the size of an orange, and just
let them to walk out of Africa,
to mainland Asia, where they
will drift on rafts to the shores
of some Indonesian paradise.
Dwarfism is common on islands
and I like thinking of our miniature
ancestors, surrounded by water,
in the years before their extinction,
when they walked among
crocodiles and tortoises,
enjoyed red crater lakes,
ridges, river canyons.
Let them lie down in the cool
shelter of time where they will
be discovered by a Catholic priest,
who won't be believed;
let them be mistaken for children,
and called hobbits, but let them
be real: their fires rising, smoke
I can still see, from this distance,
in the ancient, moonless night.

Northwest Passage

For centuries explorers dreamed of it: a route
from Europe to the far East, elusive passage

from Atlantic to Pacific. I speak of desire,
a river running through the imagination,

a shortcut over the top of the world.
For these expeditions Victorians invented

the Boat-Cloak: an inflatable dinghy
that doubled as a jacket, moved by

a sail that was also an umbrella.
Sir John Franklin's ships were named

Erebus and Terror and they disappeared
looking for it: 128 men, two thousand books,

five tons of chocolate. Sometimes I imagine
Lewis and Clark searching for that ladder

of myths, Henry Hudson cast adrift
by a mutinous crew. I think of icebergs

as tall as night rising from a violent
black sea, and the eerie music

they made rubbing against one another,
screams and groans: a Siren song.

No Windows

No windows in the grocery store where the food
is already dead and does not deserve
a view and no windows in the topless bars
where women undress for money.
No windows in the waiting room
where patients wish their name would
never be called: just a television mumbling
to itself and a stack of unappetizing magazines.
No windows in the examination room
where my mother first heard the word cancer;
no windows anywhere for days after she knew.

The End of the War

In train stations soldiers arrive, their heads
leaned out windows, hands reaching

through smoke for the lives they left behind.
Men in uniform kiss women in dresses

on city streets, lean them back so they are like
stalks of flowers

remembering the wind; in my grandparents' album
one uncle carries his girlfriend through a garden,

leaves trembling, her skirt alive.

The Woman in the Viagra Commercial

She is meant to make men feel like having sex:
a flower in her hair, idle in a treehouse
in some distant, tropical paradise where men get
and keep an erection. When she speaks she barely

moves her face and afterwards she saunters
through an evening in which she is giddy and flirtatious,
lounging in a dress that clings. The woman in the commercial
is supposed to make men more comfortable talking

to their doctors about Viagra, though she also mentions
the possibility that the pill will cause them to lose
their hearing or vision, the chance that their erection
will never cease and they will end up in

an emergency room, their excitement clinically ridiculous.
Crickets sing in the Viagra commercial and the treehouse
is too beautiful for children though it reminds me
of the summers when I climbed into a leafy green

canopy and forgot the world below, summers
when I refused to descend though the night
deepened. The commercial makes me
sad for men and women, for the way women stand

around in short skirts, with blossoms in their hair,
the way men get old and find themselves
in need of a pill, or at least contemplating one,
in the thickening foliage of time, sad for the way

sex becomes another kind of medical emergency,
another reason to talk to your doctor.

Childbirth Class

Class took place in an abandoned building:
industrial carpet, dark offices
with locked doors. Our teacher

wore her hair in a bun; she had
a plastic pelvis she pulled
from a bag: removable uterus, fallopian tubes,

huge head of a baby, waiting to crown. I remember,
in particular, two tattooed teenagers
in Def Leppard t-shirts, the fat pillows we used

to practice relaxation. Each class concluded
with a movie of a lady in labor: legs spread,
face sweaty. Once,

my husband and I skipped the lecture
and went to eat meat instead:
pork chops, steak, lamb on a stick.

Near the end, a classmate bragged
that her cervix was dilating, and our teacher
reached her hand into a plastic vagina

like a magician. I was afraid
of childbirth, yet I liked rolling around
on the floor with my swollen tribe,

liked the way we breathed
until we were as vast as an ocean.

Bamboo Forest

My mother meant to hide from the neighbors
which is why she planted an island of bamboo

in the middle of our yard, why it raged
like fire over a nearby fence, threatening

all that was tidy and civilized. At night
I could hear it growing: the music

of disappearances, of privacy
ripening; these were not trees but strange,

miraculous grasses that longed
to expand: ignoring boundaries and

property lines, searching for the appetites
of Pandas and rats.

Overcoat, Stones

Bombs exploded her home in Bloomsbury;
bombs went off in her mind. After finishing

a draft of her last novel, Virginia Woolf found
she was too sad to read; voices interrupted

her sleep, her dreams; she left two letters,
filled her overcoat with stones,

abandoned her hat and cane by the banks
of the Ouse River. A rush of currents

carried her out of that day in late March,
through weeks, to a distant bridge where

school children played.

Adam and Eve in Couples Therapy

The therapist tells Adam that he should let go of his anger
at Eve for talking him into the fruit; he made
his own decision and, anyway, it's all in the past
where nothing can be changed. Eve says that paradise
was a form of ignorance and Adam says

maybe, but he liked it there, beneath the blossoms,
unaware of his own nudity. Eve tells Adam
that their sons crave emotional guidance,
that Cain is angry and in need of a father's attentions;
Adam tells Eve that she has no judgment, no ability

to follow instructions, and Eve tells Adam
that he doesn't understand her curiosity,
her hunger for knowledge. Eve tells Adam
that his relationship to God is unhealthy,

that he needs to think for himself, set boundaries.
Then, the therapist asks them each to say something
positive and Adam says he likes the way the animals
are quiet now, how they stand, pensive, sniffing in fields,
and Eve says she enjoys the fires they build

together at night, the way Adam gathers wood
and they take turns rubbing two sticks together,
hard, until they are hot.

Potter's Field

In potter's field there are a thousand babies
in plain pine boxes: strangers

or paupers, unclaimed remains.
If no one writes your dates on a stone

are you forgotten? Maybe you drowned
off the coast of nowhere, or maybe you fell

from a great height. Are you still falling?
Probably you grew old and your relatives

lived in another country; probably you
were born too soon. Did you spend

all your money on a cure? In potter's field
the babies are babies, just quieter;

they drink night instead of milk, recede
instead of growing; they cannot walk

so they are learning to be still.

You're Never Prepared

You're never prepared for the ending:
the Titanic rearing up like a horse

while passengers fall, their cries
like the wings of crickets

in late summer, or the Hindenburg
on its evening descent into Lakehurst:

fabric fluttering, moorings dropped,
the beginning of a blue flame.

The dog turns her head away
from the chicken you've torn

from the bone; Rhett tells Scarlett
he doesn't give a damn.

The ending: Babe Ruth on his last trip
to the ball field, using his bat to help him stand.

The Royal Menagerie

I will tell you, then, of the white bear
who lived at the end of a leash and fished
in the river Thames, of the leopard that stole

parasols and tore them to pieces,
the monkeys that enjoyed a furnished room,
the zebra who drank ale and visited

a canteen. Rulers exchanged
exotic animals and they arrived in London
from the far reaches of the known world;

beasts roamed the royal tower
where they ate nails, nibbled the limbs
of visitors. Like their royal owners

they were dangerous and sad, able to delight
and frighten. They dreamed sometimes
of the places from which they were taken:

lush jungles, African savannas,
deep green forests of rain.

The Rich Are Preparing for the End of the World

The rich are preparing for the end of the world;
they've built fifteen story apartment complexes

inside missile silos, purchased vacation homes
in New Zealand, wooded land in the Pacific Northwest;

they're fortifying bunkers and buying
a lifetime supply of contact lenses, solar panels,

generators, guns; the rich are worried
about the possibilities: crashing financial markets,

natural disasters, bombs, plagues, wars.
They believe in the apocalypse

so they're taking classes in archery, investing
in precious metals, ordering extra passports,

a million freeze dried dinners, salty peas in cans.

1911 Triangle Shirtwaist Factory Fire

Sparked by discarded cigarettes, fire began
on the eighth floor of the Asch Building

and ascended to the tenth; flames fed by cotton
and paper ignited just before five hundred young

women went home for the night; this was a gentle
spring and most evenings workers walked

down the stairs, through Washington Square,
to the doors of their own glowing

tenements. It took fifteen minutes
for smoke to smother the rooms where girls

hunched over sewing machines; some gathered
beside locked doors where they waited

for help that never came; others climbed
to a rooftop where they hoped to use a ladder

as a bridge; a dozen held hands
on a ledge: fire wild behind them,

iron fences rising below.

Penelope's Bed

Her headboard was also an olive tree: alive
in the bedroom, at the center of the house,

where it thickened and grew. The weather
of her marriage was recorded in its rings --

days of rain, days of drought,
nights when she was alone, waiting

for her husband to come home.
For twenty years Odysseus wandered

and Penelope opened cold sheets,
watched the leaves flutter above.

He landed on islands
and slept with women in caves;

he listened to Sirens sing; but Penelope
was expected to be faithful: weaving

and unweaving her future,
her desire patient in the shade.

Penelope's bed was the place where
she waited and we do not know

if she dreamed of sex or adventure,
if she ever hung from a branch,

or popped an olive in her mouth;
I think of her rolling over

in the dappled light, of her hand,
reaching.

Sanatoriums

The cure depended on big meals served
with milk and sunlight, on the healing air

of mountaintops or towns by the sea.
Patients were supposed to sit, among pillows,

in front of picture windows, or on open porches,
even in winter; in sepia photos

you find them lounging in chairs,
on verandas, covered with snow.

Death was removed from the architecture:
no mortuaries or gravestones,

no funeral homes, no grief. Instead,
there were walks through forests,

lonely cottages, horseback rides.
Patients were forbidden to drink wine

or fall in love; they could not speak
of the blood in their handkerchiefs, of the way

they were consumed by fever and dread.
In one, corpses were lowered at night, by cable,

to a waiting train which snaked through
darkness, smoke rising behind.

Giraffe in a House of Bats

Sea otters hold hands when they sleep,
hoping not to drift apart, and whales,
eternally watchful, rest one half

of their brains at a time. Migrating
birds pause in the air, amid pillows
of clouds, and elephants prefer to stand.

Consider the giraffe and bat: one asleep
for two hours, while the other dangles,
upside down, for twenty. Chimps build

beds in the canopies of Ironwood trees,
while baboons are natural insomniacs:
fretful and restless. In my childhood cottage,

my mother could not sleep; we sank
into night, our eyes closed, while she
wandered with foxes and mice; the sound

of her feet on the stairs was
the sound of the sea. Even now, I find her
in the kitchen, stirring chocolate

into moonlit milk, see her sitting
in front of black and white movies;
she was a giraffe in a house of bats,

her neck endless.

Watching *The Blob* With My Daughter

My daughter is doing homework one afternoon when The Blob
begins its descent into a small town: gelatinous, devouring
a doctor and a mechanic; it oozes down the aisles
of a grocery store, visits a theater, all the time growing

larger. The police try to kill The Blob by dropping
a power line on it, but in the end, only the cold
will destroy it, which is why an air force jet drops it

into the North Pole. My daughter imagines what might
happen next: elves swallowed, Santa's ruined workshop,
polar bears erased from the drifting white. The Blob,

I tell my daughter, must be the 1960s, which lurked
just beyond the suburbs of that movie: long hair, communes.
The Blob was hippies and LSD, was Woodstock

and my parents protesting Vietnam. The Blob was me:
born before my mother finished college, gestating
through her art history class, where the professor's slides
moved from the pretty dots of the Impressionists

to the mystery of Surrealism.

Extinct

Gone the way Dodos are gone
because they lacked flight or suspicion;
gone like the Pigfooted Bandicoot, hopping
through the sands of a distant Australian night;
gone the way Passenger Pigeons are gone,

though they once darkened the skies;
vanished like the Woolly Mammoths
when their vast grassy plains became
pine forests, like the Carolina Parakeets

who would not abandon a wounded
member of their flock, like Stellar's Sea Cows
who nibbled kelp, in the Arctic,
without teeth. That last summer I went
home to the island, the one my father

incorporated, and his office was dusty,
his dog asleep; even his law books turned
their backs; time became a change
in the weather, a new predator.

Playing With Fire

I moved a napkin
through a candle's flame while my mother
dressed for a dinner party. I left her upstairs,

in front of a mirror, and found the table
set for guests: plates like faces,
wine glasses, two candles, blooming.

My mother opened a bottle of perfume
and I reached my hand towards the fire,
which seemed alive, like I was. Later,

my hermit crab slept beneath
a shell, and my mother stood
in a closet, where her shoes were arranged

in silent pairs. Each breeze through
the window caused the flame
to sway and, even now, my hand

is a moth.

My Mother's First Sculptures

There was an animal graveyard on the north side
of her grandfather's farm and it was here
that my mother began digging up the bones of cows
and goats, soaking them

in bleach until they were as white
as a winter moon. With wire and glue,
she practiced her articulations. She didn't know
animal anatomy and sometimes the head
of one creature appeared on the body

or legs of another. Already, death worried her.
She had known most of the beasts
she dug up from that mud, in particular
a pig she named Judith Carol and pushed
in a perambulator like a baby. Still, the bones

were confusing. I think of the barn
where she worked on her sculptures:
the big, hinged doors that opened
into a room that smelled of hay.

Sometimes cats drifted down from the loft
to watch her, bent over the particulars
of her losses, coaxing them
to stand.

Two Days Before Christmas

Two days before Christmas, my grandfather died.
You may remember the red carpet
of the funeral home, the way his tree stood

in the living room, blinking. Each holiday
my aunts gathered around the piano
and, after Thanksgiving, my grandmother's
miniature village was placed

on its white cotton winter:
tiny ice skaters orbiting a pond
beside a hill where children never stopped
sledding; her village

had thatched cottages, a town hall, a church
with candles in the windows. A mile away
a hole was being dug
while, upstairs, my grandfather's bed waited

for his return. There was no snow,
and carolers moved through the neighborhood,
in their dark robes, knocking.

My Grandmother, Swimming

She grows younger as she walks down the stairs,
the skirt of her bathing suit like the skirts

she wore after the war, when
her hair was black. For a moment she slips

into the photo I keep on my desk
where she stands under a tree at the edge

of dusk, her head on my grandfather's shoulder,
all her brothers still alive. My grandmother

lives alone in her house of memories:
antique clock, framed brides smiling

behind veils. In this blue lane she moves
slowly, not wanting to reach the end.

White

After a certain point, everything disappears in the snow
that has blown over our meadow. Behind our house,

trees become the color of piano keys and our breath
opens. I am already tired of this part of my life:

moon canoe in a lake of cold stars. The church we pass
each evening is white, and the sails on my childhood

sailboat were white, leaned against a salt sky.
The sheets my grandmother hung on her clothesline

whiten in memory, bleached by time. Here
I find myself walking again, in drifts, with a lantern

that swings over the winter I cannot leave behind.

With Animals

Like Romulus and Remus, let us be suckled
by the she-wolf, but never discovered

by the shepherd; let's slip
into the forest before the village

can teach us words. Let's live
with the monkeys, like the Ugandan boy

who fled his house when his mother
was murdered by his father,

and found the green canopies
of time. Let the wild dogs rescue us

from our cardboard box and teach
us how to sniff: our teeth sharp,

our eyes luminous in the dark.
We'll remember how

to eat leaves, and freedom, and roots.
There was once a girl in a mountain den

who became a bear, a boy, abandoned
by his mother, who grew feathers,

a naked child no one can catch
who, I swear, still gallops with gazelles.

The Zoo

We went to the zoo in that August heat,
watched African vultures

sleep under gray wings, saw
a Cheetah balanced on a fallen branch,

visited the small mammal house where curiosity
grew whiskers and a tail. Later, the Komodo dragon

soaked himself in a pond, while an anteater
searched the earth with his pendulous snout.

In a year our daughter would leave us
and the great apes reached their

dark hands through the bars, searching
for fruit.

What You Can Do With a Ruined Uterus

You cannot use it as a raft or place it in the sky
like a cloud. There is no way to attach it to a pole
at the end of the driveway like a mailbox.

A ruined uterus will not grow a head and tail
and purr in the evenings; it cannot be given legs
and used as a table; it will not fly like a kite.

It won't come when you call it
and it won't stand in the window singing
like a bird. You cannot plant a garden in it

or wear it like a hat. When my mother's uterus
was ruined they threw it away in a hospital
where the floors were scrubbed and the place

where I was made became barren.
When my uterus failed it was buried under
flesh, where no one could see.

You can't pack a ruined uterus like a suitcase
and you can't teach it to read. It might be
a hammock for a spider in a haunted house.

It might be a boat without an ocean.

Shark Attacks

There was the man who went swimming at twilight
off the coast of Whale Head Bay, his watch
still ticking on the porch of his rental cottage;

he washed up in pieces: his hand under
a fishing pier, his foot sunk in sea grass.
One woman was swimming with dolphins

alongside a line of buoys, in a wet suit,
when a Great White tore her leg. Off Oak Island
two children lost their left arms and, in Hatteras,

a man was bitten between rib cage and hip
while wading in waist-high water. After this,
the summer sounded like helicopters hovering

over our coast, like worry and searching. Scientists said
the water was too salty and sea turtles
were nesting in record numbers; they said

the wind changed direction and blew
fish closer to shore. It was sudden and troubling:
we knew sharks didn't mean to eat us,

yet they ate. It was a case of mistaken identity:
sharks imagining a surfboard, for instance, as the belly
of a seal. I had watched them in aquariums

with my husband: their frozen eyes and
jagged mouths, gray gills and fins. Before it all
happened I got trapped inside a wave

that held me down; I let a current carry me
too far off shore. Where were the sharks that afternoon?
Did they know who I was?

Old Woman Returns to Rosebank Avenue

She had grown up in our row house,
could remember the day a glass chandelier

was hung in our dining room, knew
which door upstairs opened to a balcony

with a red railing, balanced over a garden
of Orchids that bloomed only at night.

She knew the trees in our yard before they
reached above our rooftops, when

it was possible to sit in their canopies
and watch men with hats walk home

from factories; I do not know where she
came from, with her white hair

and broken umbrella, or where
she went after she knocked on our door

and stepped inside to see it all one
last time: crystal doorknobs,

the bedroom where she once closed
her eyes, the closet in which her father

measured her steady ascent.

Melting Ice

For seventy-five years they slept together in ice,
dressed in clothes from 1942, near a book,
a backpack, a watch; they were a shoemaker
and a teacher, gone out to milk cows
in the Swiss Alps, and they never came home,
their seven children waiting
while windows darkened,
an aunt crying at the bottom of the stairs.
Wife and husband fell in a crevasse and did not live
to see their sons become bakers, stonemasons,
priests. Instead, snow and ice
like a veil, they remained
hidden until a ski lift operator, walking
in the mountains, off a trail, above a resort,
noticed two black stones in the shape
of people, walking between Valais and Bern,
leaned into the wind.

My Mother's Van

Even now it idles outside the houses
where we failed to get better at piano lessons,
visits the parking lot of the ballet school

where my sister and I stood awkwardly
at the back. My mother's van was orange
with a door we slid open to reveal
beheaded plastic dragons and bunches

of black, half-eaten bananas; it was where
her sketchbooks tarried among
abandoned coffee cups and

science projects. She meant to go places
in it: camp in its back seat
and cook on its stove while

painting the coast of Nova Scotia,
or capturing the cold beauty of the Blue Ridge
mountains at dawn. Instead, she waited
behind its wheel while we scraped violins,

made digestive sounds
with trumpets, danced badly at recitals
where grandmothers recorded us

with unsteady cameras. Sometimes, now,
I look out a window and believe I see it,
see her, waiting for me beside a curb,

under a tree, and I think I could open the door,
clear off a seat, look at the drawing in her lap,
which she began, but never seemed to finish.

Radioactive Boars

I read about them, in Japan,
after the nuclear disaster.
While other animals -- monkeys,
rats -- got cancer
wild boars prospered: stood on stout legs,
under fur, their snouts proud.
They multiplied, spread through
abandoned farms and villages,
snorting. Forgive me for admiring
their sturdiness and adaptability
as they wandered down
from radioactive mountains.
They tottered through a noxious
snow, ate tainted vegetables,
slept under wilted trees.
I want to be more like them,
you understand, want to rise up
on unlikely hooves.

Elegy for Thomas Lux

I was his student so I know he would want this poem
to have a title, and I'm sure he would
like me to include the words *pajamas* and *birdbath*;
he wore jeans and converse sneakers
with a jacket and tie and his great mane
of blonde hair, in memory, falls forward.
I knew his public self: the one that made
introductions and explained onomatopoeia,
but I knew, too, that he loved his daughter,
Claudia, and softball, because I was on
his team, and when we practiced he realized
I could make home runs if he reminded me
of Elizabeth Bishop while I was at bat. Lux said:
do not fear the bad poem, which will
be forgotten, but the doily poem
which will find its way into the best journals
because it is empty but well crafted.
He filled his classes with construction
workers, judges, former dentists
and housewives; he did not care about
diplomas, paperwork, stupid rules,
did not want to read about things
that happened in your bathroom,
did not advise describing your apartment
as a *hovel;* I know he preferred
the Holiday Inn to a room in a manor,
that he gave teaching jobs to
people without any experience because
he trusted their writing, that his father
delivered milk in glass bottles to doorsteps
at dawn. When he read poetry aloud
he sometimes closed his eyes, and if I
could just walk back through time
to his office, if he could be sitting
at his desk, beside a red rug, writing

with his left hand; if he could
look up, for a moment, gesturing for me
to step inside, I would show him
how closely I listened, how much I still
want to please him; he'd notice
I didn't end this poem with
an abstract idea but relied instead
on this image: Thomas Lux, a man,
in a room of books, grateful to make a living
discussing the things he loved;
he would be glad I learned to arrange
these final details: his head like a lion's,
his last name which, in Latin,
will always mean light.

Blue Elvis

It was August 1977 when Elvis Presley fell
face down on his Graceland bathroom floor;
by the time paramedics arrived, he was

cold and blue. I knew this because I was with
my grandmother, Belle, who called her sister,
Geraldine, who came over at once so we

could watch the news. My grandmother knew
Elvis liked peanut butter on white bread
with American cheese, eaten in his jungle room

which had Tiki chairs, fur lampshades,
a waterfall. Other neighbors arrived:
women in short skirts, women who

brought with them more of the food Elvis
loved: coconut cakes, fried chicken, bacon.
Elvis was dead, and summer had been so

hot the things we touched burned our hands:
handles of garden hoses, car doors,
the metal swing set my grandfather

built for me on the back lawn. I listened
to the sound of southern women's voices
expressing disbelief; they said *I swan*

and I pictured something rippling
and solitary; they said *Well, shut my mouth* and
I saw blue Elvis, falling.

Dressing The Kittens

I loved

the smell of their fur which was tinged
with the mystery of forests, sometimes
my father's cologne. I had

a perambulator in which the mildest one
allowed himself to be pushed: a tabby
with gray eyes; I kept him

beside me at night, his purr like a boat
in a lonely ocean. I dressed my kittens in hats,
in shoes they chewed off their feet.

I wanted to instruct them; they leapt
from the table during tea parties, refused
to join me in the bath, sharpened their claws

while I read aloud.

King Arthur on The Isle of Avalon

Mortally wounded in his battle with Mordred,
Arthur was taken by barge to the Isle of Avalon,
land of apples and grapevines, entrance
to the otherworld, place where his sword
was forged. Here he was tended by Morgana
on a golden bed where he did not die,
and winter never fell. This was the version
of the myth I preferred as a child: Arthur
not dead but hidden beyond marshlands
and mists, in fields that needed no plow,
among women who were sometimes animals.
When our mountain is surrounded by fog
we drift in a white lake and I look out
at the apple trees and the rippling,
high meadow and believe again in Arthur,
who belongs to the past and future,
like everyone I have loved.

Clocks are Stopped

Now I understand why clocks are stopped
and mirrors covered, why there are

hair wreaths and grief rings. I know why
Queen Victoria went on wearing black

for decades, why a dog continued to meet
his owner's train each afternoon though

his owner would never arrive. I find myself
pouring over mourning photographs

in which the living pose with the dead,
who have collapsed in chairs or coffins;

in one, a mother holds her daughter
in her lap beside a window, sunlight

disturbing the darkest room; the child's eyes
are shut and her nightgown seems

diaphanous; the mother's face is as soft as sand
and you can see how vast her daughter

has become, how even Atlas would have
struggled to hold her.

Robots

Perhaps you have heard of the robot in Russia,
designed to learn and overcome obstacles, who twice

abandoned the lab where he was constructed:
sliding into traffic, cars swerving

around his escape. Then, there
was the robot in Austria, meant for housework,

who, after picking up spilled cereal, became
suicidal, lighting a house on fire. There were

other robots like the Russian escapee, so what
made him so determined? What arrangement

of wires or impulses caused him to follow
those polished hallways, in search of an exit?

It seems particularly intelligent to hate
housework, to feel an ambivalence

towards the intentions of scientists, to look
out windows and notice your own wheels

are like the wheels of automobiles. I love
that robots are individuals, despite the uniformity

of their making, that if they can learn,
they can also protest.

Elephants, Grieving

You have seen, perhaps, the photographs
of elephants beneath a wide African sky,
on open grasslands, standing over

the bones of their dead: granite gray,
eyes damp, as they touch
a skull with their trunks; some

carry brush to cover what weather
and predators have exposed. In third grade
my teacher kept a dozen stone elephants

on her desk, used their legs as paperweights.
Each day we are closer to death
she told us; while we struggled to memorize

multiplication tables, her elephants observed,
unblinking, from a man-made savanna
on which they made no progress. I learned

later that elephants were poached
for their tusks, that they grew depressed
in circuses and zoos; I read about

a man, Lawrence Anthony, who saved
a herd of rogue elephants and when
he died of a heart attack his

herd traveled two days to stand
at his window, saying goodbye.
Have I told you my third grade teacher

did not live to be old? When you
died I thought of Anthony's elephants
walking in a grave procession

over the plains, their stiff legs
raising dust from the earth.

Persephone's Pomegranate

She was stolen, you understand, from a meadow,
by a man in a black chariot,
driven through darkness to the land of the dead;
she was a girl, running through sunlight; then,
she was someone's wife, sleeping among
Weeping Willows, the sound of a river

in her veins. When she first held
the pomegranate she noticed
its red skin, its shape which was voluptuous,
and, tearing it open, she saw the seeds
which were like the seeds inside herself:
finite, bloody. What did she know

about the rules of hunger? Desire was something
that happened around her: to her mother
or husband, to the shades who arrived
all day, by boat, with coins under their tongues.
She sat with Cerberus, at the gates, her hand

on one of his three heads, and remembered
the way it tasted to eat seeds, remembered
how bright the fruit had seemed
in that windowless night.

Houdini's Escapes

For instance the one from a giant milk can
filled with water; or the escape

from a Chinese water torture cell.
He escaped from chains,

straitjackets, crates. Buried six feet under,
without a casket, he clawed his way

to the earth's surface. Stripped
and restrained, he freed himself

from jail cells. Imagine him
wearing handcuffs inside a box,

dropped into the East River. He swallowed
keys, I'm told, practiced in the bath tub,

where he held his breath for days.
Surely he would have known how

to get out of unhealthy relationships
and PTA meetings, how to

cancel a holiday with enemies.
I wish I could ask him how he

did it because every escape requires
its own courage and dexterity;

every escape is also a show.

Apple Trees in Winter

Acres of apple orchards ripened in the valley beyond
North Mountain and I came to know them

the way I knew the cows that rested
beside our stream in August, swatting flies

with their tails, or the bearded goats that ate
our fields and dreamed in caves. Low and stout

those trees climbed, in rows, behind fences,
and I was intoxicated by the froth of their blossoms:

as white as a swan's feathers, their beauty
too heavy for branches; I expected the apples

that swelled in autumn, then fell,
but was surprised by the same trees

in winter, glazed with ice, beneath a new
moon: windblown, old. They reminded

me of my grandmother, before
she died, drinking water in bed,

beside a window of stars, her arms sharp.

Subterranean

All that first year I imagined my grandfather underground
though I did not want to. While we went on:
wanting things, breathing the ghostly December air,

going to dinner in places where someone refilled
our water glasses, he was down there in his box
of history. Sometimes I imagined the worms

of silence, sometimes the roots of trees reaching
for his bones. We drove our cars on mountain roads,
paid bills, and gained weight, while he moved

deeper into the mystery of his coffin. My daughter
made her way through chemistry and calculus
and our dogs grew old; one no longer leapt onto

our bed at night but slept instead on the floor,
her nose in a galaxy of dust. We went
to the movies, and a darkness fell

over us: we were glowing spectators, reaching
into the winter of our popcorn, while my grandfather
was in a different theatre, where the movie

was already over, the seats filling with time.

Tintype of Four Girls Mourning a Dead Dog

The dog lies in the foreground, on his side,
his nose in the hem of a girl's dress. It seems

as if he might be sleeping but he is
too heavy; one girl rests her hand

on his flank, near the stillness
of his tail; everyone refuses to look

into the camera's lens and each
wears a hat, as if the day began

happily; one, in profile, holds
the Irish Heath she found in a meadow

of heather, where nothing wags,
or sniffs, and nothing

will come when she calls his name.

The Death of Marilyn Monroe

The sound of wind chimes over her blue pool;
Eunice, the housekeeper, restless

at three in the morning; a locked bedroom door;
a light that had not been turned out; Marilyn Monroe

naked in bed, cradling a telephone receiver, a bottle
of Nembutal on her bedside table; the missing water glass;

the tap in the bathroom running dry;
Happy birthday sung to Jack Kennedy

in Madison Square Garden; Doctor Engleberg
knocking; a divorce from Arthur Miller;

the movie from which she'd been fired;
her window broken with a fireplace poker;

Marilyn murdered by communists;
Marilyn killed by the CIA; Marilyn, the victim

of a mafia hit; the sound of wind chimes over
her blue pool; Eunice, the housekeeper,

calling an ambulance; lights.

It's Later Than You Think

after the quotes found on clocks

Already, trees are casting shadows
in another world; you missed dinner,

and, though you have been running,
your train left the station; the smoke

of departure hangs in the air. It's later
than you think: shops closed,

winter thickening; the party died
down hours ago and now,

in the fireplace, ashes gather.
An hour passes slowly, but the years

go by quickly. Night, shortly.
It's later than you think.

Anne Sexton's Final Drive

On the night she did not die Anne Sexton
wore a red dress and waded into the Charles River,

waist-high in water, washing down pills
with a thermos of milk; this turned out to be a rehearsal

for the evening, months later, when
she removed her rings and slipped into

her mother's fur coat. It was October
in Boston -- sharp air, deepening leaves --

and Anne drank Vodka in her garage,
inside her vintage Cougar, driving

towards the end of the world, her radio playing.

Plath's Last Night

Near midnight
Sylvia rang a neighbor's bell,

asking for stamps, stood
too long in the hallway, lights on,

lost in a dream; she poured
cups of milk, opened a window,

left a note with her doctor's name
and number taped to a baby carriage.

Months before, she ripped out
her phone line when a rival

called Ted, burned
her second novel, and now,

after flu and snow, it was February
on Fitzroy Road, where Yeats once dreamed;

she sealed her kitchen with tape
and towels, little ripped dishcloths.

My Parents, Young

She stands on thin legs adjusting
the antennae of our television set,

though no picture is ever clear,
and he just finished law school;

last week a dentist told him that, at twenty five,
he has the mouth of an old man. They have

a dog, Hambone: his ears drag through
grass in a park where they will push

me into the stars on a wooden swing.
She has taken a picture of me

on the laps of grandparents who will
die, one after another, after astronauts

land on the moon: Helen whose sons
didn't come home from war,

Lucius who is too weak to speak,
Joseph in his rocking chair, beyond

the fig trees, smoking.

Blackbeard's Treasure

You know where it's buried: off the coast of childhood,
under salt and time; he named his stolen flagship
Queen Anne's Revenge, wore a silk sling

of pistols, a hat lit with fuses, a beard that continues
to grow. I was told he killed no one until his final
battle, yet he disrupted the trans-Atlantic commerce

of three empires, haunted my dreams by swimming,
headless, through the shallow inlets of my mind.
He married a local girl, was drinking

on our beaches the night before the Royal Navy
came for him in their sloops without cannons,
ready for hand to hand combat; I searched for his

treasure with cousins: our guesses on maps
I still find in hat boxes, and I have gone on searching
in towns without oceans, without sand.

Jonestown

I was a child, so it was the children I thought of,
in a remote commune, off the coast of South America,
forced to call Jim Jones *father*. Evenings,

when my own father took off his business suit to drink
scotch and watch the news, I listened to the stories
of disobedient Jonestown children, forced

to spend the night at the bottom
of wells, or locked in plywood boxes;
I knew they were learning to be compliant.

Anyone who tried to escape the cult
was drugged; the Jonestown children lived in huts
woven from Troolie Palm and many

suffered fevers; before they drank
the Kool-Aid laced with cyanide they were called
from bed, during an exercise called white nights,

asked to line up and swallow a cup
of juice without asking questions.
I was asked to line up too, all the time, at school.

I was a child, so it was the children I thought of,
and they were the first to die, opening their mouths
for parents or nurses, in a pavilion, in the middle

of a jungle, in the trembling tropical afternoon.

In 18th Century Britain

It was fashionable for owners of country estates
to have a hermit living in their garden grotto:

unwashed, hair growing long. He was paid
to go barefoot, or recite poetry for party guests,

asked to sit in silence at a desk in a hut
with a skull, a book, an hourglass. The hermit

was supposed to embody melancholy
in his druid costume, with his unclipped

fingernails, and he lived in solitude among
ponds and flower beds, his presence unmanicured.

Gardens became less geometric, more free-form,
and a hermit was hired to live in a state

of contemplation, at the edge of a deep woods,
near a shed full of rakes and spades,

beyond ladies in pale silk gowns, taking tea.

Automat, 1927

after the painting by Edward Hopper

The woman in the green coat must have come in
from the cold to drink coffee at a marble table,
alone. Night has blackened the window

behind her but the lights of the automat
are reflected in glass, floating over
the swelling of her hat, her downcast eyes,

her bare legs, crossed. I have always loved
the idea of the automat:
food, eternally new, displayed like jewels

in compartments, released by coins,
and coffee, brewed fresh every twenty
minutes, flowing from brass dolphin heads.

Edward Hopper's woman is sitting
in polished solitude, wearing one glove,
and New York has vanished behind her;

she holds a cup the color of winter
and the other diners, unseen, are lost
in the snow of their own thoughts:

Wall Street's crash two years in the future,
nickels in their pockets.

A Pirate at Midlife

At midlife, Stede Bonnet grew tired of his wife
and children so he built a ship with a library,
named it *Revenge*. He left behind

his sugar plantation in Barbados, swaying
under the sun, and became a pirate
though he knew nothing of sailing.

This is midlife: the nagging wife, the plantation
growing thirsty at noon. Bonnet was a terrible
pirate but he did meet Blackbeard

and, for a moment, was his partner,
which involved walking around
his hero's deck in a nightshirt, recovering

from a lost battle by reading a book.
Bonnet died two years after he went to sea
but, before he was hanged, he learned

to fire cannons, quit paying his crew,
realizing, finally, that money made them lazy.
He was pardoned for awhile by Governor Eden

who lived in the town beside my grandfather's cottage,
just beyond the river of my childhood, and I
liked the drawings of Bonnet in my storybook of pirates

with his fancy jacket and powdered wig. I knew
nothing yet of middle age, of the desire
for excitement before death. I used my crayons

to decorate a picture of Bonnet's children:
waving to him from fields of sugar, while he
raised a Jolly Roger and floated away.

Bear In My Car

I found a bear in my car: opening a bag of cookies,
my purse flung in the grass. He liked

my station wagon, not my husband's jeep,
visited when I parked under the Blue Spruce

and forgot to lock the door. The bear was big,
having slumbered several seasons in a cave

made of waiting, and once he ripped open my seat,
carried my mail into the forest,

as if delivering it to squirrels. The bear
stepped out of winter and opened

the door to my life, then practiced
driving on West Virginia back roads:

through valleys and hollows, his paws
like my hands.

Baby Cages

In those days little city apartments
were considered too stuffy for babies

so a portable cage was invented.
Infants were suspended from open windows

in bonnets and sweaters or, in summer,
without any clothes. Fresh air was required

to purify the blood and exposing children
to cold weather was supposed

to improve immunity. In London,
under smog, wire cages were attached

to tenant buildings, one brand
boasting an insulated roof. In photos, caged

babies float over trees and avenues, amid
pigeons and windows, on blankets, clutching

rattles. They might be wingless angels
caught in lobster pots, featherless birds

imprisoned in the sky.

FAITH SHEARIN is the author of five previous books of poetry: *The Owl Question* (May Swenson Award), *The Empty House, Moving the Piano, Telling the Bees,* and *Orpheus, Turning* (Dogfish Poetry Prize). Her work has been read aloud on *The Writer's Almanac* and included in Ted Kooser's *American Life in Poetry.* She has received awards from the National Endowment for the Arts, The Barbara Deming Memorial Fund, and The Fine Arts Work Center in Provincetown. She lives with her husband and daughter in a cabin on top of a mountain in West Virginia.

CPSIA information can be obtained
at www.ICGtesting.com
Printed in the USA
LVHW01s0313090518
576519LV00001B/5/P